Shapcott. lyr Wensley

The Story of Bethlehem

a short cantata for Christmas services

Shapcott. lyr Wensley

The Story of Bethlehem
a short cantata for Christmas services

ISBN/EAN: 9783741192272

Manufactured in Europe, USA, Canada, Australia, Japa

Cover: Foto ©Thomas Meinert / pixelio.de

Manufactured and distributed by brebook publishing software
(www.brebook.com)

Shapcott. lyr Wensley

The Story of Bethlehem

NOVELLO'S ORIGINAL OCTAVO EDITION.

THE

STORY OF BETHLEHEM

A SHORT SACRED CANTATA

FOR CHRISTMAS SERVICES, &c.

THE WORDS WRITTEN BY

SHAPCOTT WENSLEY

THE MUSIC COMPOSED BY

JOHN E. WEST.

Price One Shilling and Sixpence.
Tonic Sol-fa, One Shilling.

LONDON: NOVELLO AND COMPANY, LIMITED

AND

NOVELLO, EWER AND CO., NEW YORK.

LONDON :
NOVELLO AND COMPANY, LIMITED,
PRINTERS.

THE STORY OF BETHLEHEM.

I.

Bethlehem, O Bethlehem !
Not least art thou among fair Judah's princes.
For out of thee a ruler shall come forth,
And He shall be the shepherd of my people.

II.

O'er Salem's towers and Zion's steep,
 The peaceful moonlight reigns ;
And shepherds fold their flocks to sleep,
 On Bethlehem's star-lit plains.

Now hushed is every earthly sound
 Beneath the solemn skies ;
In stillness deep, in peace profound,
 The world expectant lies.

O holy night ! Blest hour sublime !
 Thou gift divine and free !
The troubled heart through endless time,
 Shall turn with joy to thee.

More blest by far than kings of might,
 Are Judah's lowly swains,
Who watch their flocks this holy night,
 On Bethlehem's silent plains.

III.

O lonely watchers through the silent hours,
Uplift your eyes ! A growing glory breaks,
More fair than all the jewels of the sky ;
For shining angels bear to you this night
Sweet words of peace from heaven's Eternal
 King !

IV.

A light from the land immortal,
 All heaven with its splendour fills,
It falls on the silent watchers,
 It shines on the midnight hills.
O'erwhelmed by the wondrous glory,
 The shepherds are sore afraid ;
But the angel of God is near them,
 And bids them be undismayed.

And the message of love is spoken :
" Good tidings of joy I bring,
 Behold in the city of David,
 Is born your Saviour and King."
And lo ! with the radiant angel
 Is seen an immortal throng,
And wide through the hush of midnight,
 Is borne their celestial song.

For the beauty of heaven is beaming,
 And stars of the night grow dim,
While over the land enchanted,
 There rolls the majestic hymn,
The wonderful angel-anthem,
 Proclaiming the Saviour's birth :
" To God in the highest, glory,
 And peace and good-will on earth."

V.

Let us now go even unto Bethlehem,
And see these things which have come to pass,
Which the Lord hath made known unto us.

VI.

(From Hy. A. & M., No. 59.)

O come, all ye faithful,
 Joyful and triumphant,
O come ye, O come ye to Bethlehem ;
 Come and behold Him
 Born, the King of Angels ;
O come, let us adore Him, Christ the Lord.

God of God,
 Light of Light,
Lo, He abhors not the Virgin's womb ;
 Very God,
 Begotten, not created :
O come, let us adore Him, Christ the Lord.

Sing, choirs of Angels,
 Sing in exultation,
Sing, all ye citizens of heaven above :
" Glory to God
 In the highest " ;
O come, let us adore Him, Christ the Lord.
                                        Amen.

VII.

In Bethlehem's ancient city,
The infant Saviour lies,
The mother is bending o'er him,
With love in her gentle eyes;
The mother so pure and holy,
With love in her gentle eyes.
" The Inn has no room, beloved,
Where Thou mayest lay Thy head ;
But slumber Thou here, beloved,
In peace in Thy manger bed."

O not to a stately palace,
Are Bethlehem's shepherds shown ;
For rude is the humble dwelling,
And guarded by love alone ;
Where Mary in saintly beauty,
Bends over that lowly throne :
" O calm be Thy sleep, beloved,
Though poor be Thy natal shed,
For angels of God, beloved,
Shall watch o'er Thy manger bed."

VIII.

And the shepherds made known the story
Which was told them by the angels ;
And they that heard it wondered.
But Mary kept all these sayings,
And pondered them in her heart.

IX.

Now o'er the plains at break of day,
The shepherds take their homeward way,
And fill with joy the smiling morn,
Proclaiming ever, Christ is born !

O blest are they who caught the sound,
That rent the calm of night profound ;
Who heard the herald angels sing,
Glad tidings of the new born King.

O blest of all mankind are they,
Who sought the manger where He lay ;—
On whom the gentle mother smiled,
Whilst watching near the holy child.

O happy shepherds ! earth would raise
Her song to join your fervent praise ;
And turn with hope to catch the light,
That filled your souls that wondrous night.

X.

Shepherds of Bethlehem, rejoice !
Uplift to God your grateful hearts !
Proclaim afar the wonders of His grace,
Till all the tongues of earth shall join your
songs !
In Bethlehem's city there is born this day,
A glorious Saviour, which is Christ the Lord

XI.

Rejoice, rejoice, ye nations,
And bid contention cease !
Go kneel with Bethlehem's shepherd swain
Before the Prince of Peace.
Ye kings of earthly splendour,
His mightier sway confess,
Whose glory is humility,
Whose crown is righteousness !

Ye sad and heavy laden,
Who feel the proud world's scorn,
Let hope light up your weary hearts,
For Christ the Lord is born !
All ye by sin enfettered,
All ye by grief oppressed,
O dry your eyes, and turn to Him,
And He will give you rest.

Rejoice, ye teeming cities,
Your Prince has come to reign !
Rejoice, ye islands lone and far,
That gem the azure main !
Let flowers in fragrant beauty,
Earth's desert wastes adorn,
And love be throned in every heart,
For Christ the Lord is born !

SHAPCOTT WENSLEY.

CONTENTS.

THE STORY OF BETHLEHEM.

Nº 1. INTRODUCTION, RECIT. BASS, and CHORUS.
BETHLEHEM, O BETHLEHEM.

Shapcott Wensley.

John E. West.

Adagio.

BASS SOLO. RECIT.

Andante assai. ♩ = 68.

a tempo

Beth-le-hem, O— Beth-le-hem! Not least art thou a-mong fair

Sw. *sf*

p

Ped.

Ju — dah's princes.

cresc.

For out of thee a

f

Gt. *mf*

Sw. *mf*   *cresc.*

ruler shall come forth,____ And He shall be the shep-herd of my

Ch. or Gt

p

Ped.

peo - - ple____

poco rall.

Sw.

p

CHORUS.

Soprano.
a tempo

Beth-le - hem, O— Beth-le - hem! Not least art thou a-mong fair

Alto.

Beth-le - hem, O— Beth-le - hem! Not least art thou a-mong fair

Tenor.

Beth-le - hem, O— Beth-le - hem! Not least art thou a-mong fair

Bass.

Beth-le - hem, O— Beth-le - hem! Not least art thou a-mong fair

a tempo

G! *f*

Ju - dah's princes, For out of thee a ru-ler shall come forth ——

mf cresc.

Ju - dah's princes, For out of thee a ru-ler shall come forth ——

Ju - dah's princes, For out of thee a ru-ler shall come forth ——

Ju - dah's princes, For out of thee a ru-ler shall come forth ——

f cresc.

mp
cresc.
And He shall be the shep - herd, the shep - herd of my
Ch.
p
Sw.
Senza Ped.
peo - - ple.
Tempo Imo
rit.
3
Gt. f
cresc.
ff
Ped.

O'ER SALEM'S TOWERS AND ZION'S STEEP.

Andante tranquillo. ♩ = 76.　　　　　　　legato mp

O'er Sa-lem's

p Ch. or G!
Sw.　　　　p Sw.

Ped.　　　　Ped.

cresc.

towers and Zi-on's steep　The peace - ful moon-light reigns; And shep-herds

dim.　　*pp*

fold　their flocks to sleep,　On Beth-l'em's star-lit　plains. Now hushed is ev-'ry

cresc.　　*dim.*　　*pp*

earth-ly sound　Be - neath　the solemn　skies;　In still-ness deep, in

Ch.

cresc.

peace pro-found The world ex-pect-ant lies.

poco dim. Solo. Sw.

O ho-ly night! *rit.* *Piu mosso.* Blest

Sw. Ch. or G♮ *rit.* *mp*

cresc. hour sub-lime! Thou gift di-vine and free! The

cresc. Sw. Ped. *f*

cresc. e poco a poco animato. troubled heart through end-less time, Shall turn with joy to thee, shall *ad lib.* *a tempo*

p cresc. e poco a poco animato. *colla voce*

marcato turn with joy to thee, shall turn with joy to thee, shall turn with joy __ to thee, __

More blest by far than kings of might, Are Ju - dah's low-ly

swains, Who watch their flocks this ho-ly night, On Beth - lem's si - lent

plains, __ on Beth - lem's si - - lent

Nᵒ 8. RECIT. BASS. O LONELY WATCHERS.

Andante.

O lone - ly watch - ers through the si - lent

hours Up-lift your eyes! __ A grow-ing glo - - ry breaks, More

Senza Ped.

fair than all the jew-els of the sky! __ For shin-ing

an - gels bear to you this night __ Sweet words of peace, __ sweet words of

peace __ from heaven's E - ter - - - - nal

Nº 4. CHORUS. A LIGHT FROM THE LAND IMMORTAL.

falls on the si - lent watch - - ers, It shines on the

falls on the si - lent watch-ers, _____ It shines on the

falls on _____ the si-lent watch - ers, _____ It shines on the

falls on the si - lent watch - - ers, It shines on the

mid - night hills. _____ A light _____ from the land im-

mid - night hills. _____ A light _____ from the land im-

mid - night hills. _____ A light _____ from the land im-

mid - night hills. _____ A light _____ from the land im-

- mor - tal, All heaven with its splen-dour fills, _____

- mor - tal, All heaven with its splendour fills, _____

- mor - tal, All heaven with its splen-dour fills, _____

- mor - tal, All heaven with its splen - - dour

_____ It falls on the si - lent watch - ers, _____ It

_____ It falls on the si - lent watch - ers, _____

_____ It falls on the si - lent watch - ers,

fills, It falls on the si - lent watch - ers,

cresc.
shines, it shines on the mid -
f cresc.
It shines, it shines on the mid -
f cresc.
It shines, it shines on the mid -
f cresc.
It shines, it shines on the mid -
f
cresc.
p
- night hills.
ff
A
- night hills.
ff
A
- night hills.
ff
A
- night hills.
ff
A
ff

light!

light!

light!

light! O'er-whelmed by the wondrous

Sw. mf

But the

glo - ry,____ The shepherds are sore a - fraid,____ But the

p Ch. or Sw.

angel of God is near them, And bids them be un - dis - mayed.

angel of God is near them, And bids them be un-dis - mayed.

p Sw.

ff G.t or Solo Reed.

Senza Ped.

marcato

ff

rit.

Meno mosso, maestoso.

And the message of love is spo - ken:

ff

rit.

And the message of love is spo - ken:

ff

rit.

And the message of love is spo - ken:

ff

rit.

And the message of love is spo - ken:

Meno mosso, maestoso.

ff G.t

Ped.

QUASI RECIT. Sopranos (or Soprano Solo.)
"Good ti-dings of joy I bring,
mp Sw.
a tempo
ff Gt.
Ped.
QUASI RECIT.
Be-hold in the
mp Sw.
ci-ty of Da-vid, — Is born your Sa-viour and King."
Tempo Imo
Gt. mf
Ped.
CHORUS.
And lo! with the ra-diant an-gel
And lo! with the ra-diant an-gel
And lo! with the ra-diant an-gel
And lo! with the ra-diant an-gel
cresc.
ff

sonore

Is seen an im - mor - tal throng, _____ And wide through the

sonore

Is seen an im - mor - tal throng, _____ And wide through the

Is seen an im - mor - tal throng, _____

Is seen an im - mor - tal throng, _____

f Sw.

hush of mid - night, ___ Is borne their ce - les - tial song,

hush of mid - night, ___ Is borne their ce - les - tial song,

sonore

And wide through the hush of mid - night, Is borne their ce -

sonore

And wide through the hush of mid - night, Is borne their ce -

allargando
fff
their ce - lés - - tial song,
fff
their ce - les - - tial song,
allargando
fff
- les - tial song, their ce - les - - tial song,
fff
- les - tial song, their ce - les - - tial song,
allargando
ff Gt
a tempo
poco rit.
a tempo
ff
ff
their ce - les-tial song. For the beau - -
ff
ff
their ce - les-tial song. For the beau - -
poco rit.
a tempo
ff
ff
their ce - les-tial song. For the beau - -
ff
ff
their ce - les-tial song. For the beau - -
a tempo
poco rit.
ff
ff Gt
Ped.

- ty of heaven is beam - - ing, And stars of the night grow dim, ____

- ty of heaven is beam - - ing, And stars of the night grow dim, ____

- ty of heaven is beam - - ing, And stars of the night grow dim, ____

- ty of heaven is beam - - ing, And stars of the night grow dim, ____

____ While o - ver the land en - chant - - ed, There

____ While o - ver the land en - chant - ed, ____ There

____ While o - ver ____ the land en - chant - ed, ____ There

____ While o - ver the land en - chant - - ed, There

rolls the ma - jes - tic hymn,_____ The won - -

rolls the ma - jes - tic hymn,_____ The won - -

rolls the ma - jes - tic hymn, _____ The won - -

rolls the ma - jes - tic hymn,_____ The won - -

- der-ful an-gel - an - - them, Pro - claim-ing the Sa - viour's

- der-ful an-gel - an - - them, Pro - claim-ing the Sa - viour's

- der-ful an-gel - an - - them, Pro - claim-ing the Sa - viour's

- der-ful an-gel - an - - them, Pro - claim-ing the Sa - -

cresc. poco a poco
birth: "To God in the high-est, glo - ry, to
birth: "To God in the high-est, glo - - ry, to
cresc. poco a poco
birth: "To God to God in the high-est,
viour's birth: "To God in the high - - - est,
cresc. poco a poco
God in the high-est glo - ry, to God in the highest,
God, to God in the highest, glo - - - ry,
glo - ry to God in the highest, God in the highest,
glo - - ry, to God in the highest, glo - - ry,

glo - - - ry, And peace _____

glo - - - ry, And peace _____

glo - - - ry, And peace _____

glo - - - ry, And peace _____

_____ And peace _____ and _ good - will _____

_____ And peace _____ and

_____ And peace _____ and

_____ And peace _____ and

good - will _____

good - will _____ on earth. _____ To God, _____

good - will _____ on earth. _____ To God, _____

good - will _____ on earth. _____ To God, _____

good - will _____ on earth. _____ To God, _____

_____ to God. _____

_____ to God. _____

_____ to God. _____

_____ to God. _____

poco rit.

attacca

LET US NOW GO EVEN UNTO BETHLEHEM.

Let us now go e-ven un-to Beth-le-hem,

And see these things which have come to pass, Which the

Lord hath made known un-to us

Con moto moderato e maestoso.

O COME, ALL YE FAITHFUL.

L'istesso tempo.

Tune—*"Adeste Fideles."*

O come, all ye faithful, Joyful and tri - um - phant, O

come ye, O come ye to Beth - le - hem; Come and be -

(Sop.)

O come let us a - dore Him, O

- hold Him Born, the King of An - gels;

(Ten.)

come let us a - dore Him,

come let us a - dore Him, O come let us a - dore Him, Christ the Lord.

2. God of God,
   Light of Light,
Lo! He abhors not the Virgin's womb;
   Very God,
   Begotten, not created:
O come, let us adore Him, Christ the Lord.

3. Sing, choirs of Angels,
   Sing in exultation,
Sing, all ye citizens of heaven above:
   "Glory to God
   In the highest;"
O come, let us adore Him, Christ the Lord.

A - men

* It is suggested that the last verse be sung in unison, with varied harmony in the Organ

No. 7. SOPRANO SOLO. IN BETHLEHEM'S ANCIENT CITY.

Allegretto pastorale. ♩ = 52.

In Beth-le-hem's an-cient ci - ty, The in - fant Sa - viour lies, ____ The mo-ther is bend-ing o'er ____ him, With love in her gen - tle eyes; ____ The mo-ther so pure and ho - ly, With love in her gen-tle eyes.

The Inn has no room, be - lov - ed, Where

Thou mayest lay Thy head; — But slum-ber Thou here, be - lov - ed, In

peace ___ in Thy man - - - ger bed.

O not to a state - ly pal - ace, Are

Bethlehem's shepherds shown; For rude is the hum-ble dwel - ling, And guarded by love a - lone;— Where Ma-ry in saint-ly beau - ty Bends

over that low-ly throne:— "O

calm be Thy sleep, be - lov - ed, Though poor be Thy na - tal shed,— For

an-gels of God, be - lov - ed, Shall watch — oer Thy man

Nº 8. RECIT. BASS.
AND THE SHEPHERDS MADE KNOWN THE STORY.

And the shep-herds made known the sto - ry Which was

told them by the an-gels; And they that heard it wondered.

But Mary kept all these say - ings and pondered them in her

Nº 9. CHORUS and DUET. NOW O'ER THE PLAINS.

heart. Now o'er the plains at break of day, The

Andantino quasi Allegretto. ♩ = 92.

cresc.   *f*

shepherds take their homeward way, And fill with joy the smil-ing morn, Pro-

cresc.   *mf* G♮

Man.

ff

-claim-ing ev - er, Christ is born, Christ is born, Christ is

f

Ped.

born!

Soprano. *mf*

Now o'er the plains at break of day The

Alto. *p*

The shep - - herds take their

Tenor. *p*

The shep - - herds take their

Bass. *mf*

Now o'er the plains at break of

C H O R U S.

shepherds take their homeward way, And fill with joy the

home - - ward way,___ And fill with joy the

home - - ward way,___ And fill with joy the

day The shepherds take their way, And fill with joy the

smil-ing morn, Pro-claim-ing ev - er Christ is born, Christ is born,

smil - ing morn, Pro-claim - ing ev-er Christ___ is born,

smil-ing morn, Pro-claim-ing ev - er Christ is born, Christ is born,

smil-ing morn, Pro-claim-ing ev - er Christ is born, Christ is born,

31

Christ is born!

Christ is born!

Christ is born!

Christ is born!

Bass Solo.

O

blest are they who caught the sound, That rent the calm of night profound; Who

heard the herald angels sing, Glad ti - dings of the new - born

King.

C H O R U S.

f con maestà

Glad ti - dings of___ the new - born King.

Glad ti - dings of___ the new - born King.

Glad ti - dings of___ the new - born King.

Glad ti - dings of___ the new - born King.

Gt

f

ff   *dim.*

Ped.

Tenor Solo.

mf   *Meno mosso.*   *poco cresc.*

O blest of all mankind are they, Who

Bass Solo.

mf   *poco cresc.*

O blest of all man-

rall.   *Meno mosso.*

Sw.   *p*

Ped.

sought the man-ger where He lay; On whom the gen-tle

dim.

-kind are they, Who sought the man - ger where He lay; On

dim.

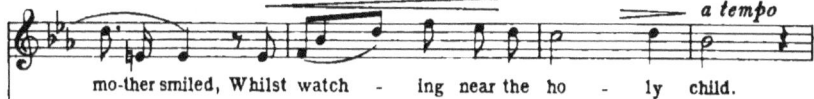

poco rall. *a tempo*

mo-ther smiled, Whilst watch - ing near the ho - ly child.

whom the gentle mother smiled, Whilst watching near the ho - ly child.

poco rall. *a tempo*
mf Gt

mp

O blest of all mankind are

mp

O

dim. Sw. *p*

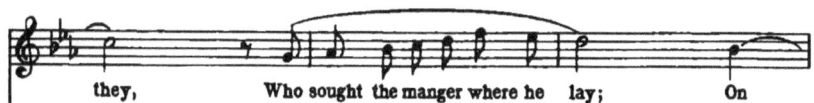

they, Who sought the manger where he lay; On

blest of all mankind are they, Who sought the manger where he

poco cresc.
dim.
whom the gen-tle mo - ther smiled,
Whilst watch-ing near the
poco cresc.
lay; On whom the gen-tle mo - ther smiled,
poco cresc.
dim.
poco rall.
a tempo
ho - ly child,
the ho - ly child.
dim.
Whilst watching near the ho-ly child,
the ho - ly child.
poco rall.
a tempo
mf
poco accel.
CHORUS.
Tempo Iº
f
cresc.
O hap-py shep - herds,
O hap-py
O hap-py shep - herds,
O hap-py shep - herds,
Tempo Iº
f
cresc.

shepherds, happy shep - herds, O hap-py shepherds! earth would

shepherds, happy shep - herds, O shep - - herds!

happy shep - herds, O shep - - herds!

happy shep - herds, O

raise Her song to join your fervent praise; And

earth would raise Her song And

earth would raise Her song And

hap-py shepherds! earth would raise Her song to join your praise; And turn with hope to catch the light, That filled your souls that

turn with hope to catch the light, That filled your souls that

turn with hope to catch the light, That filled your souls that

turn with hope to catch the light, That filled your souls that

won-drous night, filled your souls that won - drous night. O

won - drous night, that won - drous night. O

won-drous night, filled your souls that won - drous night.

won-drous night, filled your souls that won - drous night.

hap - py shepherds! earth would raise   Her   song to join your fervent

hap - py shepherds! earth would raise   Her   song to join your fervent

f grandioso

O   hap - py shepherds! earth would raise   Her

f grandioso

O   hap - py shepherds! earth would raise   Her

grandioso

cresc. e animato

praise;   And   turn with hope   to   catch the light, That

praise;   And   turn with hope   to   catch the light, That

cresc. e animato

song to join your praise; And turn with hope   to   catch the light, That

song to join your praise; And turn with hope   to   catch the light, That

cresc. e animato

filled your souls that wondrous night,_____ that filled your souls that wondrous

filled,_____ that filled your souls that wondrous night, that wondrous

filled _____ your souls, filled your souls ___ that wondrous

filled,_____ that filled your souls that wondrous night, that wondrous

ff *pesante* *marcato e poco rit.*

night,_____ that filled your souls, filled your souls __ that won-

night,_____ that filled__ your souls,__ your souls that won-

night,_____ that filled your souls, filled your souls __ that won-

night,_____ that filled your souls, filled your souls __ that won-

ff marcato

- drous night, that filled your souls that won-drous night,_____

- drous night, that filled your souls that won-drous night,_____

- drous night, that filled your souls that won-drous night,_____

- drous night, that filled your souls that won - drous night,_____

_____ that won-drous night._____

_____ that won-drous night._____

_____ that won-drous night._____

_____ that won-drous night._____

Nº 10. RECIT. BASS.
SHEPHERDS OF BETHLEHEM, REJOICE.

Shep-herds of Beth-le-hem,— re-joice!— Up-lift to God your grate-ful hearts!— Pro--claim a-far the won-ders of His grace, Till all the tongues of earth shall join your songs! In Bethlem's ci-ty there is born this day,

largamente   *Maestoso.*

A glo-rious Sa-viour,   which is Christ the Lord,

rit.   *Allegro moderato.*

Christ the Lord, Christ the Lord!

accel.   *rit. e marcato*   *ff*

Nº 11. CHORUS and QUARTET. REJOICE, REJOICE, YE NATIONS.

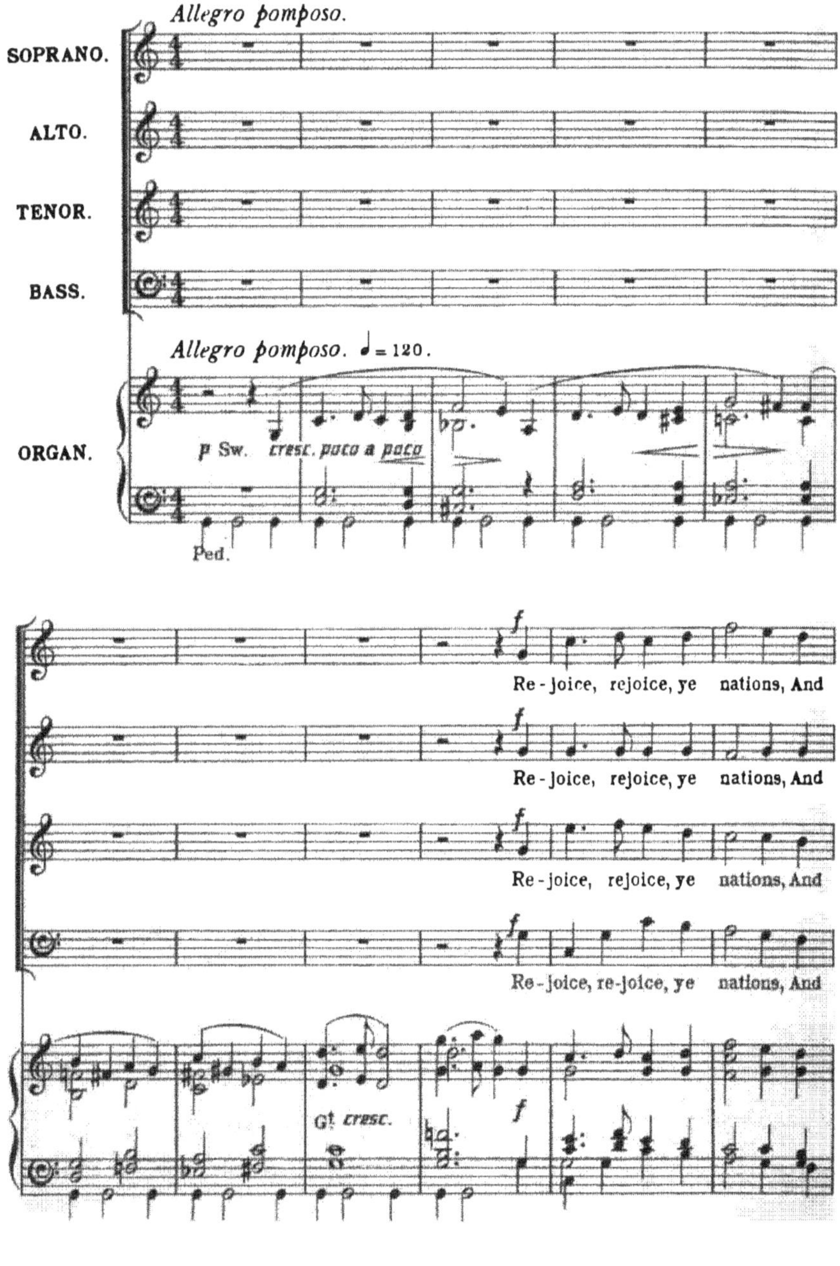

bid contention cease; Go kneel with Bethlem's shepherd swains, Before the Prince of

bid contention cease; Go kneel with Bethlem's shepherd swains, Before the Prince of

bid contention cease; Go kneel with Bethlem's shepherd swains, Before the Prince of

bid contention cease; Go kneel with Bethlem's shepherd swains, Before the Prince of

Peace. Re-joice, rejoice, ye nations, And bid con-ten-tion cease;

Peace. Re-joice, rejoice, ye nations, And bid con-ten-tion cease;

Peace. Re-joice, rejoice, ye nations, And bid con-ten-tion cease;

Peace. Re-joice, re-joice, ye nations, And bid con-ten-tion cease;— Go

mf

mf Sw.

poco stacc.

Go

Go

Go kneel with Bethle'm's shep-herd swains,

kneel with Bethle'm's shep-herd swains,

kneel with Bethle'm's shepherd swains, Be-fore the Prince of Peace, the Prince

kneel with Bethle'm's shepherd swains, Be-fore the Prince of Peace, the Prince

Be-fore the Prince of Peace, the Prince

Be-fore the Prince of Peace, the Prince

senza Ped.

— of Peace. Re - joice ye nations, re - joice ye
— of Peace. Re - joice ye nations, re - joice ye
— of Peace. Re - joice ye nations, re - joice ye
— of Peace. Re - joice ye nations, re -
f Gt
nations, re - joice.
nations, re - joice.
nations, re - joice. Ye kings of — earthly
-joice, re - joice. Ye kings of — earthly
cresc.
ff
f Sw.

Whose glo-ry is hu - mi - li - ty,

Whose glo-ry is hu - mi - li - ty,

splendour, His mightier sway con-fess,   Whose

splendour, His mightier sway con-fess,   Whose

Whose crown is righteous-ness!

Whose crown is righteous-ness!

glo-ry is hu - mi - li - ty,   Whose crown is righteous-ness!

glo-ry is hu - mi - li - ty,   Whose crown is righteous-ness!

Re - joice, rejoice, ye nations, And

Re - joice, rejoice, ye nations, And

Re - joice, rejoice, ye nations, And

Re - joice, re-joice, ye nations, And

bid contention cease; Go kneel with Bethle'm's shepherd swains, Be-fore the Prince of

bid contention cease; Go kneel with Bethle'm's shepherd swains, Be-fore the Prince of

bid contention cease; Go kneel with Bethle'm's shepherd swains, Be-fore the Prince of

bid contention cease; Go kneel with Bethle'm's shepherd swains, Be-fore the Prince of

48

Peace. Ye kings of earthly splendour, His mightier sway con-fess,

Peace. Ye kings of earthly splendour, His mightier sway con - fess, Whose

Peace. Ye kings of earthly splendour, His mightier sway con-fess,

Peace. Ye kings of earthly splendour, His mightier sway con-fess, Whose

Whose glo-ry is hu - mi - li - ty, Whose crown is

glo-ry is hu - mi - li - ty, Whose crown is

Whose glo-ry is hu - mi - li - ty, Whose crown is

glo-ry is hu - mi - li - ty, Whose crown, whose

righ - teous - ness, is righ-teous-ness! Re-joice,
righ - teous-ness, whose crown is righ - -teous-ness! Re-joice,
righ - teous-ness, whose crown is righ - -teous - ness! Re - joice,
crown is righ - - - -teous - ness! Re - joice,
ff
re-joice, re - joice.
re-joice, re - joice.
re-joice, re - joice.
re-joice, re - joice.
p

Larghetto.
legato e con espress.
SOLO (or SEMI-CHORUS.)
Ye sad and heavy la - den, Who feel the proud world's
Ye sad and heavy la - den, Who feel the proud world's
Ye sad and heavy la - den, Who feel the proud world's
Ye sad and heavy la - den, Who feel the proud world's
Larghetto.
senza Org.
cresc.
marcato
scorn, Let hope light up your weary hearts, For Christ the Lord is
scorn, Let hope light up your weary hearts, For Christ the Lord is
scorn, Let hope light up your weary hearts, For Christ the Lord is
scorn, Let hope light up your weary hearts, For Christ
cresc.

born,_____ for Christ the Lord is born! Ye sad, ye sad and weary

born,_____ for Christ the Lord is born! Ye sad, ye sad and weary

born,_____ for Christ the Lord is born! Ye sad, ye sad and weary

___ the Lord is born, for Christ the Lord is born! Ye sad, ye sad and weary

la - den, Who feel the proud world's scorn, Let hope light up your

la - den, Who feel the proud world's scorn, Let hope light up___ your

la - den, Who feel___ the proud world's scorn, Let hope light up___ your

la - den, Who feel the proud world's scorn, Let hope light up your weary hearts, For Christ the Lord,___ Christ the Lord is born! All ye by sin en-

weary hearts, For Christ the Lord,___ Christ the Lord is born! All ye by sin en-

weary hearts, For Christ the Lord,___ Christ the Lord is born! All ye by sin-

weary hearts, For Christ, for Christ the Lord is born! All ye by sin en-

-fet-ter-ed, All ye by grief op-pressed, O dry your eyes, and

-fet-ter-ed, All ye by grief op-pressed, O dry your eyes, and

-fet-ter-ed, All ye by grief op-pressed, O dry your eyes, and

-fet-ter-ed, All ye by grief op-pressed, O dry your eyes, and

turn to Him, And He will give you rest, ___ O dry your eyes, and

turn to Him, And He will give you rest, O dry your eyes, and

turn to Him, ___ And He will give you rest, ___ O dry your eyes, and

turn to Him, And He will give you rest, O dry your eyes, and

turn to Him, And He will give you rest, ___

turn ___ to Him, And He, ___ He will give you rest, *ad lib.*

turn to Him, ___ He ___ will give you

turn to Him, And He, He will give you rest,

a tempo — — — — — — — — — *dim. poco a poco*

and He will give you rest, O dry your eyes, and

dim. poco a poco

and He will give____ you rest, O dry your eyes, and

dim. poco a poco

rest,____ will give____ you rest, O dry your eyes, and turn to

a tempo — — — — — — — — *dim. poco a poco*

will give____ you rest, He____ will____

a tempo — — — — — — *dim. poco a poco*

rall. — — — *ppp*

turn to Him, And He will give you rest,____ rest.

ppp

turn, And He will give you rest,____ rest.

rall.

Him, And He will give you rest, will give you rest.____

____ give____ you____ rest,____ will give you rest.

rall.

Allegro pomposo. *(Tempo I?)*

p 8w. cresc. poco a poco

Ped.

C H O R U S

Re - joice, ye teeming ci - ties, Your Prince has come to

Re - joice, ye teeming ci - ties, Your Prince has come to

Re - joice, ye teeming ci - ties, Your Prince has come to

Re - joice, ye teeming ci - ties, Your Prince has come to

G.t cresc.   *f*

reign; Re - joice, ye is - lands lone and far, That gem the a - zure

reign; Re - joice, ye is - lands lone and far, That gem the a - zure

reign; Re - joice, ye is - lands lone and far, That gem the a - zure

reign; Re - joice, ye is - lands lone and far, That gem the a - zure main. Let flowers in fra-grant beau - ty, Earth's des-ert wastes a -

main. Let flowers in fra-grant beau - ty, Earth's des-ert wastes a -

main.___ Let flowers in fra-grant beau - ty, Earth's des-ert wastes a -

main. Let flowers in fra-grant beau - ty, Earth's des-ert wastes a -

-dorn, And love be throned in ev - ry heart,

-dorn,__And love be throned in ev - ry heart,

-dorn, And love be throned in ev - ry heart,

-dorn, And love be throned in ev - ry heart, For

For Christ the Lord is born, the Lord is
For Christ the Lord is born, for Christ the Lord is
For Christ the Lord is born, for Christ the Lord is
Christ the Lord is born, is
cresc. e poco accel.
born And love be throned in ev - ry heart, in
born And love be throned in ev - ry heart, in
cresc. e poco accel.
born And love be throned in ev - ry heart, in
born And love be throned in ev - ry heart, in
cresc. e poco accel.

rall. molto
ev - ry heart,
For
ev - ry heart,
For
rall. molto
ev - ry heart,
For
ev - ry heart,
For
rall. molto
marcato
Ped.
Moderato e maestoso. (Come Iª)
Christ the Lord is born, Christ the Lord is born,
Christ the Lord is born, Christ the Lord is born,
Christ the Lord is born, Christ the Lord is born,
Christ the Lord is born, Christ the Lord is born,
Moderato e maestoso. (Come Iª)
♩= 88.
ff

Christ is born, Christ is born, Christ the Lord,

Christ is born, Christ is born, Christ the Lord,

Christ is born, Christ is born, Christ the Lord, for

Christ is born, Christ is born, Christ the Lord,

for Christ the Lord is born,

for Christ is born,

Christ the Lord is born, for Christ is born,

for Christ is born,

ff *poco rit. e marcato*

for Christ the Lord is

ff

for Christ the Lord is

ff *poco rit. e marcato*

for Christ the Lord is

ff

for Christ the Lord is

poco rit.

a tempo

born._____

a tempo

born._____

born._____

born._____

a tempo, maestoso

rit.

NOVELLO'S ORIGINAL OCTAVO EDITIONS

OF

Oratorios, Cantatas, Odes, Masses, &c.

(Price columns: Paper Cover · Paper Boards · Cloth Gilt)

FRANZ ABT.
MINSTER BELLS (Female voices) ... 2/6
SPRINGTIME (ditto) (SOL-FA, 0/6) ... 2/6
SUMMER (ditto) ... 2/6
THE FAYS' FROLIC (ditto) ... 2/6
THE GOLDEN CITY (ditto) (SOL-FA, 0/6) ... 2/6
THE SILVER CLOUD (ditto) ... 2/6
THE WATER FAIRIES (ditto) ... 2/6
THE WISHING STONE (ditto) ... 2/6

J. H. ADAMS.
A DAY IN SUMMER (SOL-FA, 0/6) ... 1/6

T. ADAMS.
THE CROSS OF CHRIST (SOL-FA, 0/6) ... 1/0
THE HOLY CHILD (SOL-FA, 0/6) ... 1/0
THE RAINBOW OF PEACE ... 1/0

B. AGUTTER.
MISSA DE BEATA MARIÂ VIRGINE, IN C (English) (Female voices) ... 2/6
MISSA DE SANCTO ALBANO (English) ... 3/0 4/0 5/0

THOMAS ANDERTON.
THE NORMAN BARON ... 1/0 1/6
WRECK OF THE HESPERUS (SOL-FA, 0/6) ... 1/0
YULE TIDE ... 1/6 2/0 3/0

J. H. ANGER.
A SONG OF THANKSGIVING.. ... 1/6

W. I. ARGENT.
MASS, IN B FLAT ... 2/6

P. ARMES.
HEZEKIAH ... 2/6
ST. BARNABAS ... 2/0
ST. JOHN THE EVANGELIST ... 2/6

A. D. ARNOTT.
THE BALLAD OF CARMILHAN (SOL-FA, 1/6) ... 2/6
YOUNG LOCHINVAR (SOL-FA, 0/6) ... 1/6

E. ASPA.
ENDYMION ... 4/0
THE GIPSIES ... 1/0

ASTORGA.
STABAT MATER ... 1/0 1/6

J. C. BACH.
I WRESTLE AND PRAY (SOL-FA, 0/2) ... 0/6

J. S. BACH.
A STRONGHOLD SURE (Choruses only) (SOL-FA, 0/6) ... 1/0
BE NOT AFRAID (SOL-FA, 0/4) ... 0/6
BIDE WITH US ... 1/0
BLESSING, GLORY, AND WISDOM ... 0/6
CHRISTMAS ORATORIO ... 2/0 2/6 4/0
  Ditto (PARTS 3 & 4) ... 1/0
GOD GOETH UP WITH SHOUTING ... 1/0
GOD SO LOVED THE WORLD ... 1/0
GOD'S TIME IS THE BEST (SOL-FA, 0/6) ... 1/0
JESUS, NOW WILL WE PRAISE THEE ... 1/0
JESU, PRICELESS TREASURE ... 1/0
MAGNIFICAT ... 1/0
MASS, IN B MINOR ... 2/6 3/0 4/0
MISSA BREVIS, IN A ... 1/0
MY SPIRIT WAS IN HEAVINESS ... 1/0
O LIGHT EVERLASTING ... 1/0
THE PASSION (S. JOHN) ... 2/6 3/6 4/0
THE PASSION (S. MATTHEW) ... 2/6 3/0
  Ditto (Abridged, as used at St. Paul's) ... 1/6
THOU GUIDE OF ISRAEL ... 1/0
WHEN WILL GOD RECALL MY SPIRIT ... 1/0

A. S. BAKER.
COMMUNION SERVICE, IN E ... 1/6

J. BARNBY.
REBEKAH (SOL-FA, 0/9) ... 1/0 1/6 2/6
THE LORD IS KING (97th Psalm) (SOL-FA, 1/0) ... 1/6 2/0

LEONARD BARNES.
THE BRIDAL DAY ... 2/6 4/6

J. F. BARNETT.
PARADISE AND THE PERI ... 4/0 6/0
THE ANCIENT MARINER (SOL-FA, 2/0) ... 3/6 4/0 5/0
THE RAISING OF LAZARUS ... 6/6 9/0
THE WISHING BELL (Female voices)(SOL-FA, 1/0) ... 2/6

1/5/99.

BEETHOVEN.
A CALM SEA AND A PROSPEROUS VOYAGE. ... 0/6
CHORAL FANTASIA (SOL-FA, 0/3) ... 1/0
CHORAL SYMPHONY ... 2/6
  Ditto, VOCAL PART (SOL-FA, 0/6) ... 1/0
COMMUNION SERVICE, IN C ... 1/6 3/0
ENGEDI; OR, DAVID IN THE WILDERNESS ... 1/0 1/6 2/6
MASS, IN C ... 1/0 1/6 2/6
MASS, IN D ... 2/0 3/6 4/0
MEEK, AS THOU LIVEDST ... 0/2
MOUNT OF OLIVES (CHORUSES, SOL-FA, 0/6) ... 1/0 1/6 2/6
RUINS OF ATHENS ... 1/0
THE PRAISE OF MUSIC ... 1/6 2/0 3/0

A. H. BEHREND.
SINGERS FROM THE SEA (SOL-FA, 0/9) ... 1/6

WILFRED BENDALL.
A LEGEND OF BREGENZ (Female voices) ... 1/6
THE LADY OF SHALOTT (Female voices) ... 2/6
  (Ditto, SOL-FA, 1/0)

KAREL BENDL.
WATER-SPRITE'S REVENGE (Female voices) ... 1/0

SIR JULIUS BENEDICT.
PASSION MUSIC FROM ST. PETER ... 1/6
ST. PETER ... 3/0 3/6 5/0
THE LEGEND OF ST. CECILIA (SOL-FA, 1/6) ... 2/6 3/0 4/0

GEORGE J. BENNETT.
EASTER HYMN ... 1/0

SIR W. STERNDALE BENNETT.
INTERNATIONAL EXHIBITION ODE (1862) ... 1/0
THE MAY QUEEN (SOL-FA, 1/0) ... 3/0 3/6 5/0
THE WOMAN OF SAMARIA (SOL-FA, 1/0)... 4/0 6/0

G. R. BETJEMANN.
THE SONG OF THE WESTERN MEN ... 1/0

W. R. BEXFIELD.
ISRAEL RESTORED ... 4/0

HUGH BLAIR.
BLESSED ARE THEY WHO WATCH (ADVENT) ... 1/6
HARVEST-TIDE ... 1/0

JOSIAH BOOTH.
THE DAY OF REST (Female voices) (SOL-FA, 1/0) ... 2/6

E. M. BOYCE.
THE LAY OF THE BROWN ROSARY ... 1/6
THE SANDS OF CORRIEMIE (Female voices) ... 1/6
YOUNG LOCHINVAR ... 1/6

J. BRADFORD.
HARVEST CANTATA ... 1/6
THE SONG OF JUBILEE ... 1/6

W. F. BRADSHAW.
GASPAR BECERRA ... 1/6

J. BRAHMS.
A SONG OF DESTINY ... 1/0

C. BRAUN.
SIGURD ... 6/0
THE SNOW QUEEN (Operetta) (SOL-FA, 0/6) ... 1/0

A. HERBERT BREWER.
NINETY-EIGHTH PSALM ... 1/6

J. C. BRIDGE.
DANIEL ... 3/6
RESURGAM ... 4/0
RUDEL ... 4/0

J. F. BRIDGE.
BOADICEA ... 2/6
CALLIRHOË (SOL-FA, 1/6)... 2/6 3/0 4/0
HYMN TO THE CREATOR ... 1/0
MOUNT MORIAH ... 2/6
NINEVEH ... 2/6 3/0 4/0
ROCK OF AGES (Latin and English)(SOL-FA, 0/4)... 1/0
THE CRADLE OF CHRIST ("Stabat Mater Speciosa") ... 1/6
THE FLAG OF ENGLAND (SOL-FA, 0/9) ... 1/6
THE FROGS AND THE OX (SOL-FA, 0/3) ... 1/0
THE INCHCAPE ROCK ... 1/0
THE LORD'S PRAYER (SOL-FA, 0/6) ... 1/0

DUDLEY BUCK.

THE LIGHT OF ASIA	8/0	3/6	5/0

EDWARD BUNNETT.

OUT OF THE DEEP (130th Psalm) ...	1/0	—	—

W. BYRD.

MASS FOR FOUR VOICES	2/6	—	—

CARISSIMI

JEPHTHAH	1/0	—	—

J. D. CARNELL.

SUPPLICATION	6/0	—	—

GEORGE CARTER.

SINFONIA CANTATA (116th Psalm) ...	2/0	—	3/6

WILLIAM CARTER.

PLACIDA	2/0	2/6	4/0

CHERUBINI.

FOURTH MASS, IN C	1/0	1/6	2/6
REQUIEM MASS, C MINOR (Latin and English)	1/0	1/6	2/6
SECOND MASS, IN D MINOR... ...	2/0	2/6	3/6
THIRD MASS (Coronation)	1/0	1/6	2/6

E. T. CHIPP.

JOB	4/0	—	—
NAOMI	2/0	—	—

HAMILTON CLARKE.

DRUMS AND VOICES (Operetta) (Sol-fa, 0/9)	2/0	—	—
HORNPIPE HARRY (Sol-fa, 0/9) ...	2/6	—	—
PEPIN THE PIPPIN (Operetta), both Notations	2/6	—	—
(Ditto, Sol-fa, 0/9)			
THE DAISY CHAIN (Operetta) (Sol-fa, 0/9)...	2/6	—	—
THE MISSING DUKE (Operetta) (Sol-fa, 0/9)	2/6	—	—

S. COLERIDGE-TAYLOR.

HIAWATHA'S WEDDING-FEAST ...	1/6	—	—

FREDERICK CORDER.

THE BRIDAL OF TRIERMAIN (Sol-fa, 1/0)	2/6	—	—

SIR MICHAEL COSTA.

THE DREAM	1/0	—	—

H. COWARD.

THE STORY OF BETHANY (Sol-fa, 1/6) ...	2/6	3/0	—

F. H. COWEN.

A DAUGHTER OF THE SEA (Female voices) ...	2/0	—	—
(Ditto, Sol-fa, 1/0)			
A SONG OF THANKSGIVING... ...	1/6	—	—
CHRISTMAS SCENES (Female voices) (Sol-fa, 0/9)	2/0	—	—
DREAM OF ENDYMION... ...	2/6	—	—
ODE TO THE PASSIONS	2/0	—	—
RUTH (Sol-fa, 1/6)	4/0	4/6	6/0
ST. JOHN'S EVE (Sol-fa, 1/6) ...	2/6	3/0	4/0
SLEEPING BEAUTY (Sol-fa, 1/6) ...	2/6	3/0	4/0
SUMMER ON THE RIVER (Female vv.) (Sol-fa, 0/9)	2/0	—	—
THE ROSE OF LIFE (Female voices) (Sol-fa, 0/9)	1/0	—	—
THE WATER LILY	2/6	—	—
VILLAGE SCENES (Female voices) (Sol-fa, 0/9)	1/6	—	—

J. MAUDE CRAMENT.

I WILL MAGNIFY THEE, O GOD (145th Psalm)...	2/0	—	—
LITTLE RED RIDING-HOOD (Female voices) ...	2/0	—	—

W. CRESER.

EUDORA (A dramatic Idyll)	2/6	—	—

W. CROTCH.

PALESTINE	2/0	3/6	5/0

W. H. CUMMINGS.

THE FAIRY RING	2/6	—	—

W. G. CUSINS.

TE DEUM	1/6	—	—

FÉLICIEN DAVID.

THE DESERT (Male voices)	1/6	2/0	—

H. WALFORD DAVIES.

HERVÉ RIEL	1/0	—	—

P. H. DIEMER.

BETHANY	4/0	—	—

M. E. DOORLY.

LAZARUS	2/6	—	—

F. G. DOSSERT.

COMMUNION SERVICE IN E MINOR ...	2/0	—	—
MASS, IN E MINOR	3/0	—	—

LUCY K. DOWNING.

A PARABLE IN SONG	2/0	—	—

F. DUNKLEY.

THE WRECK OF THE HESPERUS ...	1/0	—	—

ANTONIN DVOŘÁK.

COMMUNION SERVICE, IN D	2/6	—	—
MASS, IN D	2/6	—	—
PATRIOTIC HYMN...	1/6	—	—
Ditto (German and Bohemian Words)	3/0	—	—
REQUIEM MASS	6/0	6/0	7/6
ST. LUDMILA	6/0	6/0	7/6
Ditto (German and Bohemian Words)	8/0	—	—
STABAT MATER	2/6	3/0	4/0
THE SPECTRE'S BRIDE (Sol-fa, 1/6)	3/0	3/6	5/0
Ditto (German and Bohemian Words)	6/0	—	—

A. E. DYER.

ELECTRA OF SOPHOCLES	1/6	2/0	—
SALVATOR MUNDI	2/6	—	—

H. J. EDWARDS.

PRAISE TO THE HOLIEST	1/6	—	—
THE ASCENSION	2/6	—	—
THE EPIPHANY	2/0	—	—

EDWARD ELGAR.

CARACTACUS	3/6	4/0	5/
KING OLAF (Sol-fa, Choruses only, 1/6) ...	3/0	—	5,
TE DEUM AND BENEDICTUS ...	1/0	—	—
THE BANNER OF ST. GEORGE (Sol-fa, 1/0)	1/6	—	—
THE BLACK KNIGHT	2/0	—	—
THE LIGHT OF LIFE (Lux Christi) ...	2/6	—	—

ROSALIND F. ELLICOTT.

ELYSIUM	1/0	—	—
THE BIRTH OF SONG	1/6	—	—

GUSTAV ERNEST.

ALL THE YEAR ROUND (Female vv.) (Sol-fa, 0/9)	2/6	—	—

A. J. EYRE.

COMMUNION SERVICE IN D ...	1/0	—	—

T. FACER.

A MERRY CHRISTMAS (Sol-fa, 0/6)	1/0	—	—
RED RIDING-HOOD'S RECEPTION (Operetta)...	2/6	—	—
(Ditto, Sol-fa, 0/9)			

E. FANING.

BUTTERCUPS AND DAISIES (Female voices) ...	2/6	—	—
(Ditto, Sol-fa, 1/0)			

HENRY FARMER.

MASS, IN B FLAT (Latin and English) (Sol-fa, 1/0)	2/0	2/6	3/

MYLES B. FOSTER.

SNOW FAIRIES (Female voices) ...	1/6	—	—
THE ANGELS OF THE BELLS (Female voices)...	1/6	—	—
(Ditto, Sol-fa, 0/6)			
THE BONNIE FISHWIVES (Female vv.) (Sol-fa, 0/9)	2/6	—	—
THE COMING OF THE KING (Female voices)	1/6	—	—
(Ditto, Sol-fa, 0/6)			
THE LADY OF THE ISLES ...	1/6	—	—

ROBERT FRANZ.

PRAISE YE THE LORD (117th Psalm) ...	1/0	—	—

NIELS W. GADE.

CHRISTMAS EVE (Sol-fa, 0/6) ...	1/0	1/6	—
COMALA	2/0	2/6	4/
ERL-KING'S DAUGHTER (Sol-fa, 0/9) ...	1/0	1/6	2/
PSYCHE (Sol-fa, 1/6)	2/6	3/0	4/
SPRING'S MESSAGE (Sol-fa, 0/3) ...	0/9	—	—
THE CRUSADERS (Sol-fa, 1/0) ...	2/0	2/6	4/
ZION	1/6	—	—

HENRY GADSBY.

ALCESTIS (Male voices)	4/0	—	—
COLUMBUS (Male voices)... ...	2/6	—	—
LORD OF THE ISLES (Sol-fa, 1/6) ...	2/0	—	—
ODE (for s.s.a.)	1/0	—	—

F. W. GALPIN.

YE OLDE ENGLYSHE PASTYMES ...	1/6	—	—

G. GARRETT.

HARVEST CANTATA (Sol-fa, 0/6) ...	1/0	—	—
THE SHUNAMMITE	3/0	—	—
THE TWO ADVENTS	1/6	—	—
LA BELLE DAME SANS MERCI ...	1/0	—	—

R. MACHILL GARTH.

EZEKIEL	4/0	—	—
THE WILD HUNTSMAN	1/0	1/6	—

A. R. GAUL.

AROUND THE WINTER FIRE (Female voices) ...	2/0	—	—
A SONG OF LIFE (Ode to Music) (Sol-fa, 0/6) ...	1/0	—	—
ISRAEL IN THE WILDERNESS (Sol-fa, 1/0) ...	2/6	3/0	4/
JOAN OF ARC (Sol-fa, 1/0) ...	2/6	3/0	4/
PASSION SERVICE	2/6	3/0	4/
RUTH (Sol-fa, 1/6)	2/0	2/6	4/
THE ELFIN HILL	2/0	—	—
THE HOLY CITY (Sol-fa, 1/0) ...	2/6	3/0	4/
THE LEGEND OF THE WOOD (Female voices)...	1/0	—	—
(Ditto, Sol-fa, 0/6)			
THE TEN VIRGINS (Sol-fa, 1/0) ...	2/6	3/0	4/
TOILERS OF THE DEEP (Female voices)...	2/0	—	—
UNA	2/6	3/0	4/
(Ditto, Sol-fa, 1/0)			

FR. GERNSHEIM.
SALAMIS. A TRIUMPH SONG (Male voices) ... 1/6 — —

E. OUSELEY GILBERT.
SANTA CLAUS AND HIS COMRADES (Operetta) 2/0 — —
(Ditto, Sol-fa, 0/6)

F. E. GLADSTONE.
PHILIPPI ... 2/6 — —

GLUCK.
ORPHEUS (Choruses, Sol-fa, 1/0) ... 3/6 — —
Ditto (Act II. only) ... 1/6 — —

HERMANN GOETZ.
BY THE WATERS OF BABYLON (137th Psalm)... 1/0 — —
GENIA ... 1/0 — —
THE WATER-LILY (Male voices) ... 1/6 — —

A. M. GOODHART.
ARETHUSA ... 1/0 — —
EARL HALDAN'S DAUGHTER ... 1/0 — —
SIR ANDREW BARTON ... 1/0 — —

CH. GOUNOD.
COMMUNION SERVICE (Messe Solennelle) ... 1/6 2/0 3/0
Ditto (Troisième Messe Solennelle) 2/6 — —
DAUGHTERS OF JERUSALEM ... 1/0 — —
DE PROFUNDIS (130th Psalm) (Latin Words) 1/0 — —
Ditto (Out of darkness) 1/0 — —
GALLIA (Sol-fa, 0/4) 1/0 — —
MESSE SOLENNELLE (St. Cecilia)... 1/0 1/6 2/6
MORS ET VITA (Latin or English) ... 6/0 6/0 7/6
Ditto, Sol-fa (Latin and English)... 2/0 — —
OUT OF DARKNESS ... 1/0 — —
REQUIEM MASS, from "Mors et Vita" ... 2/6 3/0 —
THE REDEMPTION (English Words) (Sol-fa, 2/0) 5/0 6/0 7/6
Ditto (French Words) ... 8/6 — —
Ditto (German Words)... 10/0 — —
THE SEVEN WORDS OF OUR SAVIOUR ON THE CROSS (Filiæ Jerusalem) 1/0 — —
TROISIÈME MESSE SOLENNELLE ... 2/6 — —

C. H. GRAUN.
TE DEUM ... 2/0 2/6 4/0
THE PASSION OF OUR LORD (Der Tod Jesu) ... 2/0 2/6 4/0

ALAN GRAY.
ARETHUSA ... 1/0 — —
SONG OF REDEMPTION ... 1/6 — —
THE FOE BEHIND ... 1/0 — —
THE LEGEND OF THE ROCK-BUOY BELL ... 1/6 — —
THE WIDOW OF ZAREPHATH ... 2/0 — —

J. O. GRIMM.
THE SOUL'S ASPIRATION ... 1/0 — —

G. HALFORD.
THE PARACLETE ... 2/0 — —

E. V. HALL.
IS IT NOTHING TO YOU (Sol-fa, 0/3) ... 0/6 — —

HANDEL.
ACIS AND GALATEA ... 1/0 1/6 2/6
Ditto, New Edition, edited by J. Barnby (Sol-fa,1/0) 1/0 1/6 2/6
ALCESTE ... 2/0 — —
ALEXANDER BALUS ... 3/0 3/6 5/0
ALEXANDER'S FEAST ... 2/0 2/6 4/0
ATHALIAH ... 3/0 3/6 5/0
BELSHAZZAR ... 3/0 3/6 5/0
CHANDOS TE DEUM ... 1/0 1/6 2/0
CORONATION AND FUNERAL ANTHEMS ... — — 5/0
Or, singly:—
LET THY HAND BE STRENGTHENED ... 0/8 — —
MY HEART IS INDITING... ... 1/0 — —
THE KING SHALL REJOICE ... 0/8 — —
THE WAYS OF ZION ... 1/0 — —
ZADOK THE PRIEST (Sol-fa, 0/1½) ... 0/8 — —
DEBORAH ... 3/0 3/6 4/0
DETTINGEN TE DEUM ... 1/0 1/6 2/6
DIXIT DOMINUS (from Psalm cx.) ... 1/0 — —
ESTHER... ... 3/0 3/6 5/0
HERCULES (Choruses only, 1/0) ... 3/0 3/6 5/0
ISRAEL IN EGYPT, edited by Mendelssohn ... 2/0 2/6 4/0
ISRAEL IN EGYPT, edited by V. Novello, Pocket Edit. 1/0 1/6 2/0
JEPHTHA ... 3/0 3/6 5/0
JOSHUA ... 3/0 3/6 4/0
JUDAS MACCABÆUS (Sol-fa, 1/0) ... 2/0 2/6 4/0
JUDAS MACCABÆUS, Pocket Edition ... 1/0 1/6 2/0
Ditto (Choruses only) ... 0/8 1/3 —
L'ALLEGRO (Choruses only, 1/0) ... 2/0 2/6 4/0
NISI DOMINUS ... 1/0 — —
O COME, LET US SING UNTO THE LORD (5th Chandos Anthem) 1/0 — —
ODE ON ST. CECILIA'S DAY ... 1/0 1/6 2/6
O PRAISE THE LORD (6th Chandos Anthem) 1/0 — —
SAMSON (Sol-fa, 1/0) ... 2/0 2/6 4/0
SAUL (Choruses only, 1/0) ... 3/0 3/6 4/0
SEMELE... ... 3/0 3/6 5/0
SOLOMON ... 3/0 3/6 5/0
SUSANNA ... 3/0 3/6 5/0

HANDEL.—Continued
THEODORA ... 3/0 3/6 5/0
THE MESSIAH, edited by V. Novello (Sol-fa, 1/0) 2/0 2/6 4/0
THE MESSIAH, ditto, Pocket Edition ... 1/0 1/6 2/0
THE MESSIAH, edited by W. T. Best (Sol-fa, 1/0)... 2/0 2/6 4/0
Ditto (Choruses only) ... 0/8 1/3 —
THE PASSION ... 3/0 3/6 5/0
THE TRIUMPH OF TIME AND TRUTH... 3/0 3/6 5/0
UTRECHT JUBILATE ... 1/0 — —

SYDNEY HARDCASTLE.
SING A SONG OF SIXPENCE (Operetta)... ... 0/6 — —

BASIL HARWOOD.
INCLINA, DOMINE (86th Psalm) ... 2/0 — —

F. K. HATTERSLEY.
ROBERT OF SICILY ... 2/6 — —

HAYDN.
FIRST MASS, IN B FLAT (Latin) ... 1/0 1/6 2/6
Ditto (Latin and English) ... 1/0 1/6 2/6
INSANÆ ET VANÆ CURÆ (Latin and English)... 0/4 — —
SECOND MASS IN C (Latin) ... 1/0 1/6 2/6
SIXTEENTH MASS (Latin) ... 1/6 2/0 3/0
TE DEUM (English and Latin) ... 1/0 — —
THE CREATION (Sol-fa, 1/0) ... 1/0 1/6 2/6
THE CREATION, Pocket Edition ... 1/0 1/6 2/0
THE PASSION; OR, SEVEN LAST WORDS OF OUR SAVIOUR ON THE CROSS ... 2/0 3/6 4/6
THE SEASONS ... 3/0 3/6 5/0
Each Season, singly (Spring, Tonic Sol-fa, 6d.) 1/0 — —
THIRD MASS (IMPERIAL) (Latin and English) 1/0 1/6 2/6
Ditto (Latin) ... 1/0 1/6 2/6

BATTISON HAYNES.
A SEA DREAM (Female voices) (Sol-fa, 0/6)... ... 2/6 — —
THE FAIRIES' ISLE (Female voices)... ... 2/6 — —

H. HEALE.
JUBILEE ODE ... 1/6 — —

C. SWINNERTON HEAP.
FAIR ROSAMOND (Sol-fa, 2/0) ... 3/6 4/0 5/0

EDWARD HECHT.
ERIC THE DANE ... 3/0 — —
O MAY I JOIN THE CHOIR INVISIBLE ... 1/0 — —

GEORG HENSCHEL.
OUT OF DARKNESS (130th Psalm) ... 2/6 — —
STABAT MATER ... 2/6 — —
TE DEUM LAUDAMUS, IN C ... 1/6 — —

HENRY HILES.
THE CRUSADERS ... 2/6 — —

FERDINAND HILLER.
A SONG OF VICTORY (Sol-fa, 0/9) ... 1/0 1/6 —
NALA AND DAMAYANTI ... 4/0 — 6/0

H. E. HODSON.
THE GOLDEN LEGEND ... 2/0 — —

HEINRICH HOFMANN.
CINDERELLA ... 4/0 — —
MELUSINA ... 3/0 2/6 4/0
SONG OF THE NORNS (Female voices) ... 1/0 — —

C. HOLLAND.
AFTER THE SKIRMISH... ... 1/0 — —

HUMMEL.
ALMA VIRGO (Latin and English) ... 0/4 — —
COMMUNION SERVICE, IN B FLAT ... 2/0 — 4/0
Ditto, IN E FLAT ... 2/0 — 4/0
Ditto, IN D ... 2/0 — 4/0
FIRST MASS, IN B FLAT ... 1/0 1/6 2/6
QUOD IN ORBE (Latin and English) ... 0/4 — —
SECOND MASS, IN E FLAT ... 1/0 1/6 2/6
THIRD MASS, IN D ... 1/0 1/6 2/6

W. H. HUNT.
STABAT MATER ... 3/0 3/6 —

G. F. HUNTLEY.
PUSS-IN-BOOTS (Sol-fa, 0/9) ... 2/0 — —
VICTORIA; OR, THE BARD'S PROPHECY ... 2/0 — —
(Ditto, Sol-fa, 1/0)

H. H. HUSS.
AVE MARIA (Female voices) ... 1/0 — —

F. ILIFFE.
SWEET ECHO ... 1/0 — —

W. JACKSON.
THE YEAR ... 2/0 2/6 —

G. JACOBI.
CINDERELLA (Sol-fa) ... 2/0 — —

D. JENKINS.
DAVID AND SAUL (Sol-fa) ... 3/0 3/6 —

A. JENSEN.
THE FEAST OF ADONIS ... 1/0 1/6 —

E. CUTHBERT NUNN.
THE FAIRY SLIPPER (Sol-fa, 0/8) ... 2/0 — —

REV. SIR FREDK. OUSELEY.
THE MARTYRDOM OF ST. POLYCARP ... 2/6 — —

R. P. PAINE.
THE LORD REIGNETH (93rd Psalm) ... 1/0 — —

PALESTRINA.
MISSA ASSUMPTA EST MARIA ... 2/6 — —
MISSA BREVIS ... 2/6 — —
MISSA "O ADMIRABILE COMMERCIUM" ... 2/6 — —
MISSA PAPÆ MARCELLI ... 2/0 — —

H. W. PARKER.
HORA NOVISSIMA ... 2/6 — —
LEGEND OF ST. CHRISTOPHER ... 6/0 — —
THE KOBOLDS ... 1/0 — —

C. H. H. PARRY.
A SONG OF DARKNESS AND LIGHT ... 2/0 — —
BLEST PAIR OF SIRENS (Sol-fa, 0/8) ... 1/0 — —
DE PROFUNDIS (130th Psalm) ... 2/0 — —
ETON ... 1/0 — —
INVOCATION TO MUSIC ... 2/6 — —
JOB (Choruses, Sol-fa, 1/0) ... 2/6 — —
JUDITH (Choruses, Sol-fa, 2/0)... 5/0 6/0 7/6
KING SAUL ... 6/0 6/0 7/6
L'ALLEGRO (Sol-fa, 1/6) ... 2/6 — —
MAGNIFICAT ... 1/6 — —
ODE ON ST. CECILIA'S DAY (Sol-fa, 1/0) ... 2/0 — —
PROMETHEUS UNBOUND ... 3/0 — —
THE GLORIES OF OUR BLOOD AND STATE ... 1/0 — —
THE LOTUS-EATERS (The Choric Song) ... 2/0 — —

DR. JOSEPH PARRY.
NEBUCHADNEZZAR ... 2/0 4/0 5/0
  Ditto (Sol-fa) ... 1/6 2/0 2/6

B. PARSONS.
THE CRUSADER ... 2/6 — —

T. M. PATTISON.
MAY DAY ... 1/6 — —
THE ANCIENT MARINER ... 2/6 — —
THE LAY OF THE LAST MINSTREL (Sol-fa, 0/9) ... 2/6 — —
THE MIRACLES OF CHRIST (Sol-fa, 0/9) ... 2/0 — —

A. L. PEACE.
ST. JOHN THE BAPTIST (Sol-fa, 1/0) ... 2/6 — —

PERGOLESI.
STABAT MATER (Female voices) (Sol-fa, 0/8) ... 1/0 — —

CIRO PINSUTI.
PHANTOMS—FANTASMI NELL' OMBRA ... 1/0 — —

PERCY PITT.
ROHENLINDEN (Men's voices) ... 1/6 — —

V. W. POPHAM.
EARLY SPRING ... 1/0 — —

A. H. D. PRENDERGAST.
THE SECOND ADVENT... ... 1/6 — —

E. PROUT.
DAMON AND PHINTIAS (Male voices) ... 2/6 — —
FREEDOM ... 1/0 — —
HEREWARD ... 4/0 — —
QUEEN AIMÉE (Female voices) ... 2/6 — —
THE HUNDREDTH PSALM (Sol-fa, 0/4) ... 1/0 — —
THE RED CROSS KNIGHT (Sol-fa, 2/0) ... 4/0 4/6 6/0

PURCELL.
DIDO AND ÆNEAS ... 2/6 — —
ODE ON ST. CECILIA'S DAY ... 2/0 — —
TE DEUM AND JUBILATE, IN D ... 1/0 — —
  Ditto (Edited by Dr. Bridge) (Sol-fa, 0/C) ... 1/0 — —
THREE SCENES, from "King Arthur" ... 1/6 — —

LADY RAMSAY.
THE BLESSED DAMOZEL ... 2/6 — —

F. J. READ.
THE SONG OF HANNAH ... 1/3 — —

J. F. H. READ.
BARTIMEUS ... 1/6 — —
CARACTACUS ... 2/6 — —
HAROLD ... 4/0 — 6/0
IN THE FOREST (Male voices) ... 1/0 — —
PSYCHE ... 5/0 — 7/0
THE CONSECRATION OF THE BANNER ... 1/6 — —
THE DEATH OF YOUNG ROMILLY ... 1/6 — —
THE HESPERUS (Sol-fa, 0/9) ... 1/6 — —

DOUGLAS REDMAN.
COR UNAM, VIA UNA ... 2/6 — —

C. T. REYNOLDS.
CHILDHOOD OF SAMUEL (Sol-fa, 1/0) ... 2/0 — —

ARTHUR RICHARDS.
PUNCH AND JUDY (Operetta) (Sol-fa, 0/6)... 1/6 — —
THE WAXWORK CARNIVAL (Sol-fa, 0/8) ... 1/6 — —

J. V. ROBERTS.
JONAH ... 2/0 — —

W. S. ROCKSTRO.
THE GOOD SHEPHERD ... 2/6 — —

J. L. ROECKEL.
THE HOURS (Female voices) (Sol-fa, 0/9) ... 2/0 — —
THE SILVER PENNY (Sol-fa, 0/9) ... 2/0 — —

EDMUND ROGERS.
THE FOREST FLOWER (Female voices) ... 2/6 — —

ROLAND ROGERS.
FLORABEL (Female voices) (Sol-fa, 1/0) ... 2/6 — —
PRAYER AND PRAISE ... 4/0 — —

ROMBERG.
THE LAY OF THE BELL (New Edition, translated by the Rev. J. Troutbeck, D.D.) (Sol-fa, 0-8) ... 1/0 1/6 2/6
THE TRANSIENT AND THE ETERNAL (Ditto, Sol-fa, 0/6) ... 1/0 — —

ROSSINI.
MOSES IN EGYPT ... 6/0 6/6 7/6
STABAT MATER (Sol-fa, 1/0) ... 1/0 1/6 2/6

CHARLES B. RUTENBER.
DIVINE LOVE ... 2/6 — —

ED. SACHS.
KING-CUPS ... 1/0 — —
WATER LILIES ... 1/0 — —

C. SAINTON-DOLBY.
FLORIMEL (Female voices) ... 2/6 — —

CAMILLE SAINT-SAËNS.
THE HEAVENS DECLARE—CŒLI ENARRANT (19th Psalm)... 1/6 — —

W. H. SANGSTER.
ELYSIUM ... 1/0 — —

FRANK J. SAWYER.
THE SOUL'S FORGIVENESS... 1/0 — —
THE STAR IN THE EAST ... 2/6 — —

C. SCHAFER.
OUR BEAUTIFUL WORLD ... 2/6 — —

H. W. SCHARTAU.
CHRISTMAS HOLIDAYS (Female voices) ... 0/9 — —

SCHUBERT.
COMMUNION SERVICE, IN A FLAT ... 2/0 — 2/6
  Ditto, IN B FLAT ... 2/0 — 2/6
  Ditto, IN C ... 2/0 — 2/6
  Ditto, IN E FLAT ... 2/0 2/6 4/0
  Ditto, IN F ... 2/0 — 2/6
  Ditto, IN G ... 2/0 — 2/6
MASS, IN A FLAT ... 1/0 1/6 2/6
Do., IN B FLAT ... 1/0 1/6 2/6
Do., IN C ... 1/0 1/6 2/6
Do., IN E FLAT ... 2/0 2/6 4/0
Do., IN F (Sol-fa, 0/9) ... 1/0 1/6 2/6
Do., IN G ... 1/0 1/6 2/6
SONG OF MIRIAM (Sol-fa, 0/6) ... 1/0 — —

SCHUMANN.
ADVENT HYMN, "In Lowly Guise" ... 1/0 — —
FAUST ... 3/0 3/6 5/0
MANFRED ... 1/0 — —
MIGNON'S REQUIEM ... 1/0 — —
NEW YEAR'S SONG (Sol-fa, 0/6) ... 1/0 — —
PARADISE AND THE PERI (Sol-fa, 1/6) ... 3/0 3/0 4/0
PILGRIMAGE OF THE ROSE... ... 1/0 1/6 2/0
THE KING'S SON ... 1/0 — —
THE LUCK OF EDENHALL (Male voices) ... 1/6 — —
THE MINSTREL'S CURSE ... 1/6 — —

H. SCHÜTZ.
THE PASSION OF OUR LORD ... 1/0 — —

BERTRAM LUARD SELBY.
CHORUSES AND INCIDENTAL MUSIC TO "HELENA IN TROAS" ... 3/6 — —
SUMMER BY THE SEA (Female voices) ... 1/6 — —
THE WAITS OF BREMEN (For Children) ... 1/6 — —
(Ditto, Sol-fa, 0/6)

H. R. SHELLEY.
VEXILLA REGIS (The Royal Banners forward go) ... 2/6 — —

8

NOVELLO'S OCTAVO EDITION OF ORATORIOS, &c.—*Continued*.

E. SILAS.
COMMUNION SERVICE, IN C ... ... 1/6 — —
JOASH ... ... 4/0 — —
MASS, IN C ... ... 1/0 — —

R. SLOMAN.
CONSTANTIA ... ... 2/6 — —
SUPPLICATION AND PRAISE ... ... 2/6 — —

HENRY SMART.
KING RENÉ'S DAUGHTER (Female voices) — 2/6 — —
(DITTO, SOL-FA, 1/0)
THE BRIDE OF DUNKERRON (SOL-FA, 1/6) ... 2/0 2/6 4/0

J. M. SMIETON.
ARIADNE (SOL-FA, 0/9) ... ... 2/0 — —
CUNNLA ... ... 2/6 — —
KING ARTHUR (SOL-FA, 1/0) ... ... 2/6 — —

ALICE MARY SMITH.
ODE TO THE NORTH-EAST WIND ... ... 1/0 — —
ODE TO THE PASSIONS ... ... 2/0 — —
THE RED KING (Men's voices) ... ... 1/0 — —
THE SONG OF THE LITTLE BALTUNG (ditto) 1/0 — —
(DITTO, SOL-FA, 0/3)

E. M. SMYTH.
MASS, IN D ... ... 2/6 — —

A. SOMERVELL.
ELEGY ... ... 1/6 — —
MASS, IN C MINOR ... ... 2/6 — —
ODE TO THE SEA (SOL-FA, 1/0) ... ... 2/0 — —
THE CHARGE OF THE LIGHT BRIGADE ... 0/9 — —
(DITTO, SOL-FA, 0/6)
THE ENCHANTED PALACE (SOL-FA, 0/9) ... 2/0 — —
THE FORSAKEN MERMAN ... ... 1/6 — —
THE POWER OF SOUND (SOL-FA, 1/0) ... 2/0 — —

CHARLTON T. SPEER.
THE DAY DREAM ... ... 2/0 — —

W. H. SPEER.
THE JACKDAW OF RHEIMS ... ... 2/0 — —

SPOHR.
CALVARY ... ... 2/6 3/0 4·0
FALL OF BABYLON 3/0 3,6 5 0
GOD, THOU ART GREAT (SOL-FA, 0/6) ... 1/0 — —
HOW LOVELY ARE THY DWELLINGS FAIR... 0/3 — —
HYMN TO ST. CECILIA ... ... 1/0 — —
JEHOVAH, LORD OF HOSTS ... ... 0/4 — —
LAST JUDGMENT (SOL-FA, 1/0) 1/0 1/6 2,6
MASS (for 5 solo voices and double choir) ... 2 0 — —
THE CHRISTIAN'S PRAYER 1/0 1/6 2/6

JOHN STAINER.
ST. MARY MAGDALEN (SOL-FA, 1/0) ... 2/0 2/6 4/0
THE CRUCIFIXION (SOL-FA, 0/9) ... ... 1/6 2/0 —
THE DAUGHTER OF JAIRUS (SOL-FA, 0/9) ... 1/6 2/0 —

C. VILLIERS STANFORD.
CARMEN SÆCULARE ... ... 1/6 — —
COMMUNION SERVICE, IN G ... ... 2/6 — —
EAST TO WEST ... ... 1/6 — —
EDEN 5/0 6/0 7/6
EUMENIDES ... ... 3/0 — —
GOD IS OUR HOPE (46th Psalm) ... ... 2/0 — —
MASS, IN G MAJOR ... ... 2/6 — —
ŒDIPUS REX (Male voices) ... ... 3/0 — —
THE BATTLE OF THE BALTIC ... ... 1/6 — —
THE REVENGE (SOL-FA, 0/9) ... ... 1/6 — —
THE VOYAGE OF MAELDUNE 2/6 3/0 4/0

F. R. STATHAM.
VASCO DA GAMA ... ... 2/6 — —

BRUCE STEANE.
THE ASCENSION 2/6 3/0 4/0

H. W. STEWARDSON.
GIDEON ... ... 4/0 — —

J. STORER.
MASS OF OUR LADY OF RANSOM ... ... 2/0 — —
THE TOURNAMENT ... ... 2,0 — —

E. C. SUCH.
GOD IS OUR REFUGE (46th Psalm) ... — 1/0 — —
NARCISSUS AND ECHO ... ... 2/0 — —

ARTHUR SULLIVAN.
FESTIVAL TE DEUM 1/0 1/6 2/6
ODE FOR THE COLONIAL AND INDIAN
EXHIBITION ... ... 1/0 — —
THE GOLDEN LEGEND (SOL-FA, 2/0) ... 3/6 4/0 5/0

T. W. SURETTE.
THE EVE OF ST. AGNES ... ... 2/0 — —

W. TAYLOR.
ST. JOHN THE BAPTIST ... ... — 4/0 —

A. GORING THOMAS.
THE SUN-WORSHIPPERS ... ... 1/0 —

E. H. THORNE.
BE MERCIFUL UNTO ME ... ... 1/0 —

BERTHOLD TOURS.
A FESTIVAL ODE ... ... 1/0 —
THE HOME OF TITANIA (Female voices) ... 1/6 —
(DITTO, SOL-FA, 0/9)

FERRIS TOZER.
BALAAM AND BALAK ... ... 2/6 —
KING NEPTUNE'S DAUGHTER (Female voices) 2/6 —
(DITTO, SOL-FA, 0/9)

P. TSCHAÏKOWSKY.
NATURE AND LOVE (SOL-FA, 0/4) ... ... 1/0 —

VAN BREE.
ST. CECILIA'S DAY (SOL-FA, 0/9) ... ... 1/0 1/6 1·

CHARLES VINCENT.
THE LITTLE MERMAID (Female voices) ... 2/6 —
THE VILLAGE QUEEN (Female voices) (SOL-FA, 0/6) 2/6 —

A. L. VINGOE.
THE MAGICIAN (Operetta) (SOL-FA, 0/9) ... 2/0 —

W. S. VINNING.
SONG OF THE PASSION (according to St. John)... 1/6 —

S. P. WADDINGTON.
JOHN GILPIN (SOL-FA, 0/8) ... ... 2/0 —

R. WAGNER.
HOLY SUPPER OF THE APOSTLES ... ... 2/6 —

W. M. WAIT.
GOD WITH US ... ... 2/0 —
ST. ANDREW ... ... 2/0 —
THE GOOD SAMARITAN ... ... 2/0 —

R. H. WALTHEW.
THE PIED PIPER OF HAMELIN ... ... 2/0 —

H. W. WAREING.
PRINCESS SNOWFLAKE (SOL-FA, 0/6) ... 1/0 —
THE COURT OF QUEEN SUMMERGOLD ... 1/0 —
THE WRECK OF THE HESPERUS ... 1/6 —
(SOL-FA, 0/6)

WEBER.
COMMUNION SERVICE, IN E FLAT ... 1/6 —
IN CONSTANT ORDER (Hymn) ... ... 1/6 —
JUBILEE CANTATA ... ... 1/0 1/6 —
MASS IN E FLAT (Latin and English) ... 1/0 1/6 2/
Do., IN G (Latin and English) 1/0 1/6 2,
PRECIOSA ... ... 1/0 —
THREE SEASONS ... ... 1/0 —

T. WENDT.
ODE ... ... 1/6 —

S. WESLEY.
DIXIT DOMINUS ... ... 1/0 —
IN EXITU ISRAEL ... ... 0/4 —

S. S. WESLEY.
O LORD, THOU ART MY GOD ... ... 1/0 —

J. E. WEST.
MAY-DAY REVELS (SOL-FA, 0/4) ... ... 1/6 —
SEED-TIME AND HARVEST (SOL-FA, 1/0)... 2/0 —

C. LEE WILLIAMS.
A HARVEST SONG OF PRAISE ... ... 1/6 —
GETHSEMANE 2,0 2/6
THE LAST NIGHT AT BETHANY (SOL-FA, 1/0) 2/0 2/6

A. E. WILSHIRE.
GOD IS OUR HOPE (Psalm 46) ... ... 2/0 —

THOMAS WINGHAM.
MASS, IN D (Regina Cœli) ... ... 3/0 —
TE DEUM (Latin) ... ... 1/6 —

CHAS. WOOD.
ODE TO THE WEST WIND ... ... 1/0 —

F. C. WOODS.
A GREYPORT LEGEND (1797) (SOL-FA, 0/6) 1/0 —
KING HAROLD (SOL-FA, 0/9) ... ... 1/6 —
OLD MAY-DAY (SOL-FA, 0/6) ... ... 1/6 —

E. M. WOOLLEY.
THE CAPTIVE SOUL ... ... 2/6 —

www.ingramcontent.com/pod-product-compliance
Lightning Source LLC
Chambersburg PA
CBHW021531270326
41930CB00008B/1193